gluten-free christmas

delicious cookies, cakes, pies,
stuffings and sauces for the perfect
festive table

hannah miles

photography by william reavell

RYLAND PETERS & SMALL
LONDON • NEW YORK

Dedication
For Alphonse Acheampong, with memories
of your first ever Christmas pudding!

Senior Designer Sonya Nathoo
Editor Kate Eddison
Commissioning Editor Stephanie Milner
Production David Hearn
Art Director Leslie Harrington
Editorial Director Julia Charles

Prop Stylist Olivia Wardle
Food Stylist Lucy McKelvie
Indexer Hilary Bird

Author's acknowledgements
A huge thanks as always to Ryland Peters & Small for
allowing me to write this deliciously festive gluten-free book –
in particular to my lovely friend Julia Charles for commissioning,
Stephanie Milner and Kate Eddison for their patient editing, and
Sonya Nathoo for the beautiful design. To Lucy McKelvie for the
beautiful food styling and to William Reavell for producing
stunning pictures – thank you all so much! Thanks to all at HHB
for always being there. To my friends and family who tasted all the
recipes – even though it was not Christmas (!) – I love you all x

First published in 2014
by Ryland Peters & Small
20–21 Jockey's Fields,
London WC1R 4BW
and
519 Broadway, 5th Floor,
New York NY 10012

www.rylandpeters.com

10 9 8 7 6 5 4 3 2

Text © Hannah Miles 2014
Design and photographs © Ryland
Peters & Small 2014

UK ISBN: 978-1-84975-557-3
US ISBN: 978-1-84975-580-1

A CIP record for this book is available from the British Library.

US Library of Congress cataloging-in-publication data has been
applied for.

Printed and bound in China

Notes
• Both British (Metric) and American (Imperial plus US cups)
are included in these recipes for your convenience, however it is
important to work with one set of measurements and not alternate
between the two within a recipe.
• All spoon measurements are level unless otherwise specified.
• All eggs are medium (UK) or large (US), unless otherwise specified.
• When a recipe calls for the grated zest of citrus fruit, buy unwaxed
fruit and wash well before using. If you can only find treated fruit,
scrub well in warm soapy water before using.
• Ovens should be preheated to the specified temperatures. We
recommend using an oven thermometer. For fan-assisted ovens,
adjust temperatures according to the manufacturer's instructions.

contents

introduction

Christmas, with its festive traditions of indulgent pastries, canapés and desserts, can be a problematic time for coeliacs/celiacs and those allergic to wheat. It is that time of year when there are so many delicious treats on offer and yet the vast majority of them contain wheat and gluten. The aim of this book is simple – to provide gluten-free alternatives to holiday classics that are tasty enough to serve not only to those who can't eat wheat and gluten, but to all your guests without anyone knowing the difference. This book will guide you through what to serve and how to avoid the gluten-free diet pitfalls.

Hidden gluten

When preparing gluten-free dishes, it is essential to check the ingredients carefully on product packaging or refer to the manufacturer to ensure that products are gluten-free. All forms of wheat, barley, rye and spelt must be avoided. This means that many flours and breads are out, as well as wheat-based products such as beer and soy sauce. Some of the products that can contain traces of gluten are baking powder, anti-caking agents (used to coat glacé/candied cherries and dried fruits, and found in some icing/confectioners' sugar), some yeasts, types of chocolate (some milk powders contain wheat) and stocks, so you need to pay particular attention when selecting these products.

Understanding gluten-free cooking

The key to successful gluten-free cooking is to understand the ingredients and their properties. Gluten gives elasticity to cake and bread doughs. Gluten-free substitutes lack this elasticity and need to be handled slightly differently. Generally speaking, gluten-free doughs and mixes require a lot more liquid than wheat-based recipes. If there is not enough liquid, the items will have a crumbly texture. Adding natural/plain yogurt, buttermilk or soured cream to cake mixtures will result in moist cakes. Pastry can be very crumbly without the elasticity of gluten and must be very carefully worked. Adding cheese to savoury pastry or cream cheese to sweet pastry can help bind the dough together. Rather than rolling the

pastry out into large sheets, which are likely to crumble when lifted, gently press small pieces of the pastry dough into the tin/pan until it is fully lined. Some gluten-free flours have a slightly bitter taste, which can affect the flavour of baked goods, so you need to make sure that each mix is packed full of flavour. All of the ingredients in this book are available in supermarkets, health food shops or online.

Avoiding contamination

One key requirement of successful gluten-free baking is to avoid cross contamination with wheat products. If you have a member of the family who is intolerant to gluten, the best solution is to remove all gluten products from the house. Where total removal is not possible, the best advice is to keep gluten-free products in sealed containers away from products containing gluten or wheat. Label everything clearly. If you have been baking with regular flour, small particles will have been released into the air during cooking, and can land on equipment, surfaces and even kitchen towels, leaving traces of gluten. It is therefore important to wipe down all equipment, surfaces and utensils thoroughly, and use clean kitchen towels and aprons. It takes a surprisingly small amount of exposure to wheat or gluten dust to make someone very ill.

Cross contamination is also possible through using appliances that are used to cook both wheat- and gluten-free products, such as toasters, baking sheets and cooling racks. It is also important to avoid putting knives and spoons that have been exposed to wheat products into butters, spreads and jams, as this can cause contamination. If practical, have separate tubs and jars marked as gluten-free.

Where to go for advice

If you believe that you may have a gluten intolerance, it is important to seek professional medical advice and there are many sources of information available to you. The Coeliac/Celiac Societies in the UK and USA are able to provide a large amount of support and guidance. There are a wide variety of books and other literature on this subject available in libraries and bookshops. Local support groups can also offer great advice on managing day-to-day life without gluten. There are also some fantastic resources available online that offer a range of information and advice. Forums exist where sufferers can communicate with each other and seek advice on all aspects of living a gluten-free life, such as when there is uncertainty over whether or not a particular ingredient named on a food packaging label is safe, as well as recipe suggestions.

canapés & party bites

cheese straws

These tangy cheese straws are the perfect accompaniment to a glass of wine at any festive party. You can vary the flavour in a variety of ways, topping with seeds or spices, or adding chopped fresh herbs or tangy blue cheese to the pastry.

160 g/1⅓ cups gluten-free
   plain/all-purpose flour,
   sifted, plus extra for dusting
100 g/¾ cup fine golden/
   yellow polenta/cornmeal
salt and freshly ground
   black pepper
2 eggs
100 g/6½ tablespoons
   butter, softened
250 g/1¾ cups finely grated
   cheddar cheese
1 teaspoon smoked paprika,
   plus extra for sprinkling
1 tablespoon cream cheese
50 g/⅓ cup pecans,
   finely chopped
poppy seeds, for sprinkling
   (optional)

*2 baking sheets, greased and
lined with baking parchment*

Makes 20

Preheat the oven to 180°C (350°F) Gas 4.

Place the flour and polenta in a bowl and mix together. Season with salt and pepper. Beat one of the eggs and add to the flour mixture, along with the butter, three-quarters of the cheddar cheese, the smoked paprika and the cream cheese. Mix together to form a soft dough using a stand mixer or whisk.

On a flour-dusted surface, roll out half of the dough using a rolling pin to a rectangle about 20 × 12 cm/8 × 5 inches in size. Cut it into 10 straws approximately 2 cm/¾ inch wide and 12 cm/5 inches long. Carefully transfer the straws to the baking sheets, using a spatula. Repeat with the remaining dough, adding a little water if it has dried out, to prevent it from cracking.

Beat the second egg, and brush over the tops of the straws using a pastry brush. Sprinkle over the chopped pecans and the reserved cheddar cheese. Add some poppy seeds, or use poppy seeds in place of the pecans, if you prefer. Season with salt, pepper and a little extra smoked paprika.

Bake in the preheated oven for 10–15 minutes, until golden brown. Remove from the oven and leave to cool on the baking sheets before serving. The straws are best eaten on the day they are made, although they will keep for up to 2 days in an airtight container.

dill and mustard blinis with smoked salmon

Topped with the delicate sea herb samphire and caviar, these blinis will add a touch of luxury to your celebrations. If you cannot find samphire, use cucumber ribbons instead.

For the blinis
200 g/1²/₃ cups buckwheat
    flour, sifted
2 teaspoons baking powder
2 eggs, beaten
1 tablespoon finely chopped/
    snipped fresh dill
1 tablespoon gluten-free
    sweet/American mustard
1 teaspoon caster/superfine
    sugar
salt and freshly ground
    black pepper
60 g/5 tablespoons butter,
    melted, plus extra for
    frying
325 ml/1¹/₃ cups milk

For the topping
30 g/1 oz. samphire
freshly squeezed juice of
    1 lemon
salt and freshly ground
    black pepper
300 ml/1¹/₄ cups crème fraîche
    or sour/soured cream
4 slices smoked salmon,
    cut into thin strips
caviar (optional)

steamer

large frying pan/skillet

Makes 28

First, steam the samphire in a steamer pan over boiling water for about 3 minutes, until it is just soft and cooked through. Place immediately into cold water, then, once cold, drain and season with the lemon juice, salt and pepper. Cover and store in the refrigerator until needed.

For the blini batter, place the flour, baking powder, eggs, dill, mustard and sugar in a bowl, and season well with salt and pepper. Pour in the melted butter and milk, and whisk to a smooth batter. Leave the batter to rest for about 30 minutes.

Melt a little butter in the frying pan and pour small ladles of batter into the pan to make circles, about 5 cm/2 inches in diameter. Cook for 1–2 minutes, until the undersides of the blinis are golden brown and small bubbles appear on the tops, then flip over with a spatula and cook for a further minute until both sides are golden brown. Remove from the pan and keep warm while you cook the remaining batter in the same way.

To serve, place the blinis on a serving plate and top each with a small spoonful of crème fraîche or sour cream. Add the lemon samphire, a strip of smoked salmon and a little caviar, if using. Serve immediately while the blinis are still warm.

mini jacket potatoes with crème fraîche and chives

These little canapés are always popular. They are quick and hassle-free to prepare for parties, as you can roast the potatoes in advance and just keep them warm until you are ready to serve. Make sure that you use very tiny new potatoes that are just one mouthful, so that they are easy for your guests to eat.

30 small new potatoes
300 ml/1 1/4 cups crème fraîche
1 teaspoon Dijon mustard
2 tablespoons finely chopped/snipped chives, plus extra to garnish
salt and freshly ground black pepper

large roasting pan

Makes 30

Preheat the oven to 190°C (375°F) Gas 5.

Place the potatoes in the roasting pan and bake in the oven for 30–40 minutes, until the potatoes are cooked through. To check that they are cooked, insert a knife into one of the large potatoes to check that it is soft inside. Remove from the oven and leave to cool slightly. Keep warm until you are ready to serve.

Place the crème fraîche, mustard and chives in a bowl, and whisk together lightly. Season to taste with salt and pepper. If you are making this in advance, place it in the refrigerator until you are ready to serve.

When you are ready to serve, cut a cross in the top of each warm potato, and place them on a serving dish or on individual spoons. Place a little of the crème fraîche mixture on top of each potato, and sprinkle with extra chopped chives to garnish. Serve immediately.

mini cornbreads topped with roasted courgettes

Golden cornbread makes an excellent base for canapés. This version is scented with tarragon, which gives the bread a delicate aniseed flavour.

For the cornbread
150 g/1 generous cup fine ground polenta/cornmeal
30 g/¼ cup gluten-free self-raising/self-rising flour
1 teaspoon bicarbonate of soda/baking soda
1 teaspoon hot paprika
284 ml/1 generous cup buttermilk
80 g/5 tablespoons butter, melted
2 teaspoons honey mustard
1 tablespoon finely chopped/snipped fresh tarragon, plus extra to garnish
1 egg, beaten
sea salt and freshly ground black pepper

For the topping
6 baby courgettes/zucchini
olive oil, to drizzle
sea salt
150 ml/⅔ cup crème fraîche

roasting pan

20-cm/8-in square cake tin/pan, greased and lined with baking parchment

decorative cookie cutter (optional)

Makes 24

Preheat the oven to 190°C (375°F) Gas 5.

Cut the ends off each courgette/zucchini, then cut in half lengthways and in half again crossways. You should have 24 small batons. Place in a roasting pan, drizzle with a little olive oil and sprinkle with sea salt. Bake in the preheated oven for 10–15 minutes until they start to caramelize, but are still firm enough to hold their shape. Set aside to cool, but leave the oven on.

Mix together the polenta/cornmeal, flour and bicarbonate of soda/baking soda, then stir in the hot paprika. In a separate bowl, whisk together the buttermilk, 50 g/3 tablespoons of the melted butter, the honey mustard, chopped tarragon and egg, and season with salt and pepper. Add to the dry ingredients and mix everything together. Pour the mixture into the prepared cake tin/pan and level the surface with a spatula. Bake in the preheated oven for 25–30 minutes, until the loaf is lightly golden brown on top.

Remove from the oven and brush the top of the warm loaf with the remaining melted butter, then sprinkle with a little more sea salt.

When you are ready to serve, cut the loaf into 24 small squares, and use a decorative cutter to create pretty shapes, if you like. Top each with a small spoonful of crème fraîche, a piece of roasted courgette and some chopped tarragon. These canapés are best eaten on the day they are made.

mango avocado salsa in chilli-spiced pastry cases

During the festive season, food is often rich and very filling. These little tarts are the perfect antidote as they are fresh and light, and have a nice spicy kick to them. If you are serving for vegetarians, you can simply omit the smoked salmon.

For the pastry
50 g/3 tablespoons butter, plus extra for greasing
190 g/1 1/2 cups gluten-free plain/all-purpose flour, sifted, plus extra for dusting
2 tablespoons cream cheese
a pinch of hot smoked paprika
grated zest of 1 lime

For the salsa
3 avocados
freshly squeezed juice of 3 limes
200 g/6 1/2 oz. smoked salmon
1 large ripe mango
3 tablespoons fresh coriander/cilantro, finely chopped
1/2 teaspoon hot smoked paprika, plus extra for sprinkling
freshly ground black pepper
salt (optional)

24 mini tartlet tins/pans, greased

baking parchment

baking beans

8-cm/3-in round cookie cutter

Makes 24

Preheat the oven to 180°C (350°F) Gas 4.

For the pastry, cut the butter into small cubes, and rub it into the flour with your fingertips. Mix in the cream cheese, hot smoked paprika and lime zest, then add a tablespoon of chilled water, and bring it all together to a soft dough with your hands. Add a little more water, if the pastry is too dry.

On a flour-dusted surface, roll out the pastry to a 3 mm/1/16 inch thickness, and cut out circles of pastry just larger than the size of your mini tartlet tins/pans. Line the tins with the pastry, pressing it in firmly with your fingertips and patching any cracks with pastry trimmings. Trim the edges neatly. Line with baking parchment, and fill with baking beans. Bake the tart cases blind for 10–15 minutes, until the pastry is golden brown. Allow to cool in the tins/pans, then remove the paper and baking beans.

Shortly before you are ready to serve, halve the avocados and remove the stones. Peel, then chop the avocados into small pieces with a sharp knife. Place in a bowl and add the lime juice. Stir to ensure all the avocado is coated in the juice; this will prevent it from discolouring. Cut the smoked salmon and mango into small pieces and add to the avocado. Stir in the coriander/cilantro and hot smoked paprika, and season well with pepper. (You can add salt, if you wish, but I find the smoked salmon adds sufficient salt.)

To serve, place a generous spoonful of the salsa into each tart case and sprinkle over a little extra paprika. Serve immediately. The unfilled pastry cases will keep for up to 3 days in an airtight container.

For the pastry
50 g/3 tablespoons butter
190 g/1½ cups gluten-free plain/all-purpose flour, sifted, plus extra for dusting
60 g/4 tablespoons caster/superfine sugar
1 egg yolk
grated zest of 1 lemon
40 g/3 tablespoons cream cheese

For the filling
100 g/²⁄₃ cup pecans, plus extra to decorate
75 g/⅓ cup caster/superfine sugar
75 g/⅓ cup soft dark brown sugar
1 teaspoon ground cinnamon
1 teaspoon pure vanilla extract
40 g/3 tablespoons butter
3 tablespoons golden/light corn syrup
1 egg plus 1 egg yolk, beaten

6-cm/2¼-in snowflake cookie cutter

24-hole mini muffin tin/pan, greased

Makes 24

mini pecan pies

These little pies can be served warm or cold. They have a heady vanilla and cinnamon caramel sauce, crunchy pecans and a buttery lemon pastry. Make them small enough to be just one mouthful.

To make the pastry, cut the butter into small cubes and rub it into the flour with your fingertips. Add the sugar, egg yolk, lemon zest and cream cheese, and mix together to a soft dough, adding a little cold water if the mixture is too dry. Wrap in clingfilm/plastic wrap, and chill for 1 hour in the refrigerator.

Preheat the oven to 180°C (350°F) Gas 4.

To make the filling, blitz the 100 g/²⁄₃ cup pecans in a food processor. Heat the caster/superfine sugar, soft dark brown sugar, cinnamon, vanilla extract, butter and syrup in a saucepan over low heat, until the sugars and butter have melted. Allow to cool for 10 minutes, then beat in the egg and egg yolk.

On a flour-dusted surface, roll out the pastry to a 3 mm/¹⁄₁₆ inch thickness. Stamp out 24 pastry rounds using the cutter, and press one into each hole of the muffin tin/pan. Do not worry if the pastry cracks; simply patch it up with pastry trimmings. Fill each pie with chopped pecans. Set aside one-third of the syrup mixture, then use the larger portion to fill the pastry cases, dividing it evenly between the pies. Decorate each pie with a pecan piece.

Bake the pies in the preheated oven for 12–15 minutes, until the filling is set. Take the pies out of the muffin tin/pan while still warm; it is easiest to do this by pushing a teaspoon down the side of each pie to lift it out. Transfer the pies to a wire rack. Heat the reserved syrup gently, then brush over the pies to glaze. Allow to cool before serving.

For the pastry

100 g/6 1/2 tablespoons butter
300 g/2 1/3 cups gluten-free
  plain/all-purpose flour, sifted
1 tablespoon dark
  muscovado sugar
1 egg yolk
100 g/1/2 cup cream cheese

For the caramel

1 can (397 g/14 oz.)
  sweetened condensed milk
50 g/3 tablespoons butter
1 tablespoon dark
  muscovado sugar
1/2 teaspoon vanilla salt or
  sea salt
2 tablespoons double/
  heavy cream

For the cream

1 ripe banana
2 teaspoons freshly
  squeezed lemon juice
350 ml/1 1/2 cups double/
  heavy cream

For the bananas

2 ripe bananas
2 tablespoons caster/
  superfine sugar

To decorate

100 g/1/2 cup caster/
  superfine sugar

8-cm/3-in snowflake cookie cutter

*2 12-hole muffin tins/pans,
greased*

baking beans

*piping bag fitted with a large
star nozzle/tip*

Makes 24

banana salted caramel tartlets

These tasty tarts are topped with beautiful spun sugar. For extra indulgence, add some edible gold leaf to the caramelized bananas.

For the pastry, cut the butter into small cubes, and rub it into the flour with your fingertips. Add the sugar, egg yolk and cream cheese, and mix to a soft dough, adding a little cold water if the mixture is too dry. Wrap in clingfilm/plastic wrap and chill for 1 hour in the refrigerator.

Preheat the oven to 180°C (350°F) Gas 4. On a flour-dusted surface, roll out the pastry to a 3 mm/1/16 inch thickness. Cut out 24 snowflake shapes using the cutter. Press one into each hole of the muffin tin/pan. Line each pastry case with baking parchment, and fill with baking beans. Bake for 12–15 minutes, until golden. Allow to cool in the tins/pans, then remove the parchment and beans.

For the caramel, heat the condensed milk, butter, sugar and vanilla salt in a saucepan over a gentle heat, until the butter and sugar have melted, stirring all the time. Increase the heat and cook, stirring constantly, until the caramel turns a deep golden brown. Remove from the heat and stir in the double/heavy cream, then leave to cool.

For the cream, mash the banana with the lemon juice in a large bowl. Add the cream, and whisk to stiff peaks. For the bananas, cut each banana into 12 slices. Lightly coat the flat faces of each slice in sugar. Heat a dry frying pan/skillet over medium heat, until hot. Place the banana slices in the pan and cook until the sugar starts to caramelize. Turn the slices over, and cook the other side in the same way. Remove from the pan and allow to cool.

To serve, place a small spoonful of caramel into each pastry case. Spoon the banana cream into the piping bag, and pipe a swirl on top of the caramel in each case. Top with a caramelized banana slice. To decorate, heat the caster/superfine sugar in a heavy saucepan. Swirl the pan, but do not stir. Watch it very carefully and as soon as the caramel is golden remove it from the heat. Allow to cool until it just becomes tacky, then dip a fork into the sugar, spin and pull away from the pan to make long fine strands. Use to decorate each tart, then serve immediately.

cookies & small treats

snowcap cookies

These cookies have powdered sugar crusts, which resemble snow-capped mountains when the cookies are baked. They are bursting with mouthwatering chocolate, and I don't think anyone would know they are gluten-free.

100 g/3 1/2 oz. plain/semisweet chocolate, melted and cooled
150 g/1 1/4 cups gluten-free plain/all-purpose flour, sifted
110 g/1 cup ground almonds
2 tablespoons baking powder
a pinch of salt
100 g/1/2 cup caster/superfine sugar
1 egg, beaten
100 g/6 1/2 tablespoons butter, softened
icing/confectioners' sugar, for dusting

2 baking sheets, greased and lined with baking parchment

Makes 18

Place the chocolate, flour, ground almonds, baking powder, salt, caster/superfine sugar, egg and butter in a large mixing bowl, and whisk together to a creamy dough. The dough will seem very soft, but don't worry; it will become firmer when chilled.

Wrap the dough in baking parchment, and chill in the refrigerator for 2 hours to set. If you are short of time, you can place the dough in the freezer for 30 minutes, until it is firm.

Preheat the oven to 180°C (350°F) Gas 4.

Divide the dough into 18 pieces, and roll them into small balls between your hands. Roll each ball in icing/confectioners' sugar so they are well coated, then place them on the prepared baking sheet, pressing down slightly with your fingers. Sift over more icing sugar, so that the tops of the cookies are coated in a thick layer of sugar.

Bake for 10–15 minutes until the cookies are just firm. Leave to cool on the baking sheets for a few minutes, then transfer to a wire rack using a spatula. Store in an airtight container for up to 3 days.

apple and cinnamon sugar cookies

Apple and cinnamon are two of my favourite flavours at Christmas. These cookies are great to serve with mulled wine on a chilly evening. The pearl sugar adds a delicious crunch to the cookies, which I like to think looks like snow.

180 g/1¹/₂ cups gluten-free
 self-raising/self-rising flour
 (see Note)
180 g/1³/₄ cups ground
 almonds
150 g/³/₄ cup demerara/
 turbinado sugar
1 teaspoon bicarbonate of
 soda/baking soda
1 teaspoon ground cinnamon
150 g/1 cup cinnamon-
 flavoured mixed sultanas/
 golden raisins and dried
 apple pieces (or plain
 mixed sultanas/golden
 raisins and dried apple
 pieces)
125 g/1 stick butter
2 tablespoons golden/light
 corn syrup
1 egg, beaten
pearl or nibbed sugar,
 to sprinkle

*2 large baking sheets,
greased and lined with
baking parchment*

Makes 12

Preheat the oven to 180°C (350°F) Gas 4.

Place the flour, ground almonds, demerara/turbinado sugar, bicarbonate of soda/baking soda, ground cinnamon and dried fruit in a mixing bowl, and stir together so that they are well mixed.

Heat the butter with the syrup in a saucepan over low heat, until the butter has melted. Allow to cool slightly, then stir into the dry ingredients with a wooden spoon. Beat in the egg to form a dough that is soft but not sticky.

Place 12 large balls of the dough on the prepared baking sheets, a small distance apart, and press down slightly with clean fingers. Sprinkle the pearl sugar over the top of the cookies and bake for 12–15 minutes, until golden brown. Remove from the oven and allow to cool on the baking sheets for a few minutes, then transfer to a wire rack with a spatula to cool completely. These cookies will keep for up to 5 days in an airtight container.

Note: Gluten-free self-rising flour is not easy to find in the US, but you can make your own. To every 1 cup gluten-free all-purpose or multi-purpose flour, add 1¹/₂ teaspoons baking powder and ¹/₄ teaspoon salt.

For the cake

60 g/generous ¹/₂ cup caster/
   superfine sugar
60 g/5 tablespoons butter,
   softened
1 egg
45 g/¹/₃ cup gluten-free
   self-raising/self-rising flour
   (see Note, page 24)
1 teaspoon baking powder
30 g/¹/₃ cup ground almonds

For the cherry filling

225 g/¹/₂ lb. fresh cherries,
   pitted and halved
60 g/generous ¹/₂ cup
   caster/superfine sugar
freshly squeezed juice of
   1 lemon
1 tablespoon kirsch, plus
   extra to assemble

For the chocolate
   mousse

100 ml/scant ¹/₂ cup double/
   heavy cream
100 g/3¹/₂ oz. plain/semisweet
   chocolate, melted
1 egg white
1 tablespoon caster/
   superfine sugar

To assemble

200 ml/³/₄ cup double/
   heavy cream, whipped to
   soft peaks
4 whole fresh cherries or
   cherries preserved in syrup

*20-cm/8-in round springform
cake tin/pan, greased and lined
with baking parchment*

Makes 4

snowy black forest cups

With cake bases, decadent chocolate mousse and sumptuous cherries, these desserts make a great alternative to a classic sherry trifle. Try serving them in glass Kilner jars or in sundae glasses.

Preheat the oven to 180°C (350°F) Gas 4.

Begin by preparing the cake, as this needs to cool before being used to assemble your desserts. In a mixing bowl, whisk together the sugar and butter until light and creamy. Beat the egg into the mixture and then gently fold in the flour, baking powder and ground almonds. Spoon the mixture into the prepared cake tin/pan and bake in the oven for 15–20 minutes, until the cake is golden brown and springs back to your touch, and a knife inserted into the centre of the cake comes out clean. Turn the cake out on to a wire rack to cool.

For the cherry filling, place the cherry halves, sugar, lemon juice and kirsch in a saucepan, and simmer for 5–10 minutes over medium heat, until the fruit is soft but still holds its shape and the liquid is syrupy. Allow to cool.

For the chocolate mousse, stir the double/heavy cream into the melted chocolate. In a separate bowl, whisk the egg white to stiff peaks, then whisk in the caster/superfine sugar. Fold the egg white mixture into the chocolate.

Cut the cooled sponge cake into small pieces and place them in the bottom of glasses or sundae dishes. Spoon some of the cherries and a little of their juice on to the cake and drizzle with a little extra kirsch if you wish. Reserve some of the cherry liquid for decorating. Place a large spoonful of the chocolate mousse on top of each base and leave to set in the refrigerator for at least an hour.

To assemble, top each glass with a spoonful of whipped cream. Drizzle with the reserved cherry liquid and top each portion with a whole cherry. Serve immediately.

For the cannoli tubes

100 g/³/₄ cups shelled pistachios, ground in a food processor, plus extra to decorate

250 g/2 cups gluten-free plain/all-purpose flour, sifted, plus extra for dusting

40 g/3 tablespoons caster/superfine sugar

a pinch of salt

50 g/3 tablespoons butter, softened

1 lemon

2 eggs plus 2 egg whites

vegetable oil, for frying

50 g/1¹/₂ oz. plain/semisweet chocolate, melted

For the filling

250 g/1 cup ricotta cheese

300 ml/1¹/₄ cups double/heavy cream

2 tablespoons icing/confectioners' sugar, sifted

1 tablespoon cinnamon sugar

1 teaspoon pure vanilla extract

100g/¹/₂ cup glacé/candied fruits, finely chopped

food processor

9-cm/2¹/₄-in round cookie cutter

cannoli tubes, greased

sugar thermometer

piping bag fitted with large open star nozzle/tip

Makes 18

cannoli

When celebrating Christmas and Thanksgiving with relatives in New York, the highlight of the meal is always traditional cannoli.

For the cannoli tubes, pass the ground pistachios through a sieve/strainer. Reblitz any pieces left in the sieve in the food processor (any large pieces will cause cracks in the pastry). Place all the pistachios, flour, caster/superfine sugar, salt and butter in a mixing bowl. Grate in the zest of the lemon, then add 2 teaspoons of the juice. Beat the two whole eggs, and add to the mixture. Whisk together to form a soft dough.

On a flour-dusted surface roll out some of the dough and cut out a 9 cm/2¹/₄ inch circle using the cookie cutter. Dust with flour and then roll into an oval shape, just shorter than the length of the cannoli tube. Using a palette knife to lift the dough, wrap it around the tube, pressing it tightly together where it joins. Repeat for the number of cannoli tubes you have. Place in the freezer for 15 minutes. Cover the rest of the dough with clingfilm/plastic wrap, until you are ready to reuse the cannoli tubes.

Place enough vegetable oil in a saucepan to make a layer deep enough for the cannoli tubes to float in. Heat the oil to 180°C (350°F). Remove the tubes from the freezer. Whisk the egg whites until frothy and, using a pastry brush, coat the whole of the dough around each tube in a thin layer of egg white. This will prevent the pastry from cracking. Place the cannoli tubes in the hot oil, in batches, and fry until the tubes are golden. Do not overfill the pan. When cooked, lift the tubes from the pan with a metal spatula and drain on paper towels. Allow to cool, then carefully slide out the cannoli tubes and wipe off any excess oil on the tubes. Repeat with the remaining dough.

To decorate, finely chop the extra pistachios. Dip each end of the cannoli in the melted chocolate, then into the finely chopped pistachios. Leave to set. For the filling, place the ricotta, cream, icing/confectioners' sugar, cinnamon sugar and vanilla in a bowl, and whisk until the cream just holds a peak. Stir in the glacé/candied fruits. Spoon the cream into the piping bag and pipe into the cannoli tubes. The unfilled pastry shells can be stored in an airtight container for up to 3 days.

For the cookies

250 g/2 cups gluten-free
   plain/all-purpose flour,
   sifted, plus extra for dusting
100 g/1 cup ground almonds
1 teaspoon bicarbonate of
   soda/baking soda
100 g/^{1}/2 cup caster/
   superfine sugar
1 teaspoon ground cinnamon
1 teaspoon ground ginger
1 tablespoon golden/light
   corn syrup
1 tablespoon black treacle/
   molasses
50 g/3 tablespoons butter,
   softened
1 teaspoon pure vanilla
   extract
1 egg plus 1 egg white
1 tablespoon icing/
   confectioners' sugar, sifted

For the decoration

250 g/2^1/2 cups royal icing
   sugar, sifted
1 teaspoon pure vanilla
   extract
gluten-free sugar decorations
edible glitter
green food colouring pen

*2 baking sheets, greased and
lined with baking parchment*

festive cookie cutters

*small round piping nozzle/tip
(optional)*

thin ribbons (optional)

Makes 18

christmas tree gingerbread cookies

'Come to my kitchen and share with me, warm gingerbread cookies and cranberry tea' are the words on my favourite festive sampler that hangs in my kitchen at Christmas, and there are few things nicer than sharing warm gingerbread with friends.

Preheat the oven to 180°C (350°F) Gas 4. Place the flour, ground almonds, bicarbonate of soda/baking soda, sugar, cinnamon and ginger in a mixing bowl, and mix well. Add the syrup, black treacle/molasses, butter and vanilla extract. Beat the whole egg and add to the mixture. Whisk together until you have a soft dough, bringing the dough together with your hands once mixed, and dusting with a little more flour if the dough is too sticky.

On a flour-dusted surface, roll out the dough to 5 mm/^{3}/16 inch thickness, and cut out cookie shapes with the cutters. Transfer the cookies to the prepared baking sheets, using a spatula. Any trimmings can be rerolled, but you will need to add a little water to them and mix into a ball of dough again, or the dough will be too crumbly.

Whisk the egg white and icing/confectioners' sugar together until foamy, then brush over the top of each cookie using a pastry brush. This will prevent the tops of the cookies from cracking during baking and will give the cookies a shiny glaze. If you want to be able to hang the cookies, cut a small hole in each cookie. This is easiest done with a round piping nozzle/tip. Bake for 10–15 minutes until just firm. Allow to cool on the baking sheets for a few minutes, then transfer to a wire rack to cool completely.

For the icing, whisk the royal icing sugar and vanilla extract with about 40 ml/ 2^1/2 tablespoons of cold water until the icing is thick and holds a peak when you lift up the beaters. If the icing is too thick, add a little more water; if too runny, add a little more icing sugar. Spread the icing on to the cookies using a round-bladed knife or palette knife, decorate with the sugar decorations and sprinkle with edible glitter. Leave to set. Once set, you can use a food colouring pen to decorate the cookies. If hanging on your tree, tie with pretty ribbons, threading through the holes. These cookies will keep for up to 5 days, if stored in an airtight container.

walnut cookies

I love to make these pretty walnut praline cookies at Christmas. They look very attractive in the shape of whole walnut shells. To make them you need to invest in a walnut cookie mould, which can be purchased from good cook shops or online.

For the walnut praline powder
100 g/^{1}/2 cup caster/ superfine sugar
100 g/1 cup walnuts

For the cookies
50 g/3 tablespoons butter, chilled
190 g/1^1/2 cups gluten-free plain/all-purpose flour, sifted
2 tablespoons mascarpone cheese
1 teaspoon ground cinnamon
1 tablespoon caster/ superfine sugar
icing/confectioners' sugar, for dusting

For the filling
50 g/3 tablespoons butter, softened
200 ml/generous ^{3}/4 cup double/heavy cream

silicon mat or baking sheet, greased

blender or food processor

walnut-shaped cookie moulds, greased

Makes 18 cookies

Begin by preparing the walnut praline powder, as the praline needs to be cooled before being used in the recipe. Place the caster/superfine sugar in a saucepan and melt over a gentle heat. Do not stir the pan while the sugar is melting, simply swirl the pan to ensure that the sugar does not burn. Cook until the caramel starts to turn a light golden brown colour and all the sugar has melted. Watch the sugar closely as it starts to melt, as the caramel can burn very easily.

Spread the walnuts out on the silicon mat or greased baking sheet, and pour over the caramel. It does not matter if all the nuts are covered. Allow to cool, then blitz to very fine crumbs in a blender or food processor to make praline powder.

Preheat the oven to 180°C (350°F) Gas 4.

In a large mixing bowl, rub the butter into the flour until the mixture resembles fine breadcrumbs. Add the mascarpone cheese, cinnamon, sugar and 1 tablespoon of the walnut praline powder, and bring the mixture together to a soft dough with your hands, adding 1–2 tablespoons cold water, if the mixture is too dry.

Press small pieces of the dough into each walnut mould, just filling each hole. Bake for 10–15 minutes, until the cookies are lightly golden. Allow to cool in the mould for a few minutes, then turn the cookies out on to a wire rack. Clean and re-grease the moulds, then repeat with the remaining dough until you have 36 walnut cookie halves.

For the filling, place the butter, remaining praline powder and double cream in a mixing bowl and whisk to a stiff mixture.

Place a spoonful of the walnut cream on the flat side of one of the cookies, and sandwich together with another cookie. Repeat with the remaining cookie halves. Serve, dusted with icing/confectioners' sugar. The unfilled cookies can be stored for 2 days in an airtight container.

christmas fancies

Fondant fancies have always been one of my favourite treats; squares of sponge covered with buttercream and topped with a glossy icing. These are truly festive with hints of brandy and cinnamon. Decorate with Christmas sugar decorations, making sure they are gluten-free.

For the cakes
115 g/7 tablespoons butter, softened
115 g/generous ½ cup caster/superfine sugar
2 eggs, beaten
85 g/⅔ cup gluten-free self-raising/self-rising flour, sifted (see Note, page 24)
1 teaspoon baking powder
60 g/⅔ cup ground almonds
1 teaspoon ground cinnamon
1 generous tablespoon buttermilk
1–2 tablespoons brandy

For the buttercream
75 g/5 tablespoons butter, softened
200 g/2 cups fondant icing/confectioners' sugar, sifted
1 teaspoon ground cinnamon
1 tablespoon buttermilk

For the glacé icing
400 g/4 cups fondant icing/confectioners' sugar, sifted
food colouring of your choice
sugar decorations

20-cm/8-in square tin/pan, greased and lined with baking parchment

Makes 8

Preheat the oven to 180°C (350°F) Gas 4.

For the sponge cake, whisk together the butter and sugar, until light and creamy. Add the eggs and whisk again. Fold in the flour, baking powder, ground almonds, cinnamon and buttermilk using a spatula or large spoon. Spoon the mixture into the prepared tin/pan, and bake for 20–30 minutes, until the cake is golden brown and springs back to your touch. Turn out on to a wire rack to cool completely.

For the buttercream, mix together the butter, icing/confectioners' sugar, cinnamon and buttermilk for several minutes, until you have a smooth, whipped icing. Using a sharp knife, slice the cake into two equal-sized rectangles by cutting it down the middle. Drizzle the brandy over one of the cake halves, and then cover with a thin layer of the buttercream. Place the second cake half on top and cover the whole cake in the buttercream, smoothing down with a round-bladed knife. Place the cake on a tray in the refrigerator for 2 hours to set.

For the glacé icing, place the fondant icing/confectioners' sugar in a saucepan with 3 tablespoons of water and a few drops of food colouring, and heat gently. The icing should be runny but still slightly thick so add a little more water gradually, if needed.

Cut the cake into 8 squares and place on a wire rack with a sheet of foil or baking parchment underneath to catch any drips. Spoon the warm fondant icing over each cake. Any icing on the foil can be reused by reheating if necessary.

Place a sugar decoration in the centre of each cake and leave to set. When the icing has set completely, cut the cakes away from the rack by sliding a sharp knife under each cake and place them in cake cases to serve. The cakes will keep for up to 5 days if stored in an airtight container.

chocolate marshmallow teacakes

Marshmallow 'teacakes' are favourites in the UK – chocolate shells filled with marshmallow and a little strawberry jam with a chocolate cookie base. These are my caramel versions. If you don't have a teacake mould you can use a silicon muffin mould instead.

For the cake
60 g/generous ¹/₂ cup caster/superfine sugar
60 g/5 tablespoons butter, softened
1 large/US extra large egg
45 g/¹/₃ cup gluten-free self-raising/self-rising flour, sifted (see Note, page 24)
1 teaspoon baking powder
30 g/¹/₃ cup ground almonds
1 tablespoon caramel sauce

To assemble
200 g/7 oz. milk/sweet or plain/semisweet chocolate (or 100 g/3¹/₂ oz. of each)
6 tablespoons marshmallow fluff
6 generous teaspoons caramel sauce

23-cm/9-in round springform cake tin/pan, greased and lined with baking parchment

6-cm/2¹/₄-in round cookie cutter

6-hole teacake mould

baking sheet, lined with baking parchment

Makes 6

Preheat the oven to 180°C (350°F) Gas 4. Begin by making the cake. In a mixing bowl, whisk together the sugar and butter until light and creamy. Beat the egg into the mixture and then gently fold in the flour, baking powder, ground almonds and caramel sauce. Spoon the mixture into the prepared tin/pan, and bake for 15–20 minutes, until the cake is golden and springs back to your touch, and a knife inserted into the centre of the cake comes out clean. Turn the cake out on to a wire rack to cool. Once cool, cut out 6 circles of cake using the cookie cutter. You will not need all of the cake.

Place the chocolate in a heatproof bowl over a pan of simmering water (or in two bowls over two pans, if you are using both types of chocolate) and simmer until the chocolate is melted. It is important to ensure that the bottom of the bowl does not touch the water. Once melted, spoon the chocolate into the teacake moulds, ensuring that each hole is completely coated in chocolate. It is best to do this by adding a layer of chocolate and allowing it to cool for a few minutes and then adding a second layer. Reserve around one-sixth of the chocolate for sealing the bottoms of the teacakes. Invert the mould on to the baking sheet, and allow the chocolate to set at room temperature, open-sides down. This will allow small chocolate rims to form.

Once the chocolate has set, invert the mould and place a spoonful of marshmallow fluff into each hole. If the chocolate has spread out so much that there is only a small opening, trim the chocolate with a sharp knife. Top the marshmallow with a teaspoonful of caramel sauce, then place a circle of cake on top, pressing the cake down so that it sits just below the top of the mould. Re-melt the reserved chocolate, then spoon it over the cakes to seal. Leave to set at room temperature, rounded-side down. When the chocolate has set, carefully press each teacake out of the mould.

The teacakes will store for up to 3 days in an airtight container at room temperature or in the refrigerator. Please note that if you store them in the refrigerator the chocolate will lose its glossy shine, but will still taste delicious.

Pistachio mincemeat

500 g/1 lb dried mixed fruit
50 g/¹/₃ cup crystallized ginger, finely chopped
grated zest and freshly squeezed juice of 2 oranges and 2 lemons
2 apples, grated
150 g/³/₄ cup caster/superfine sugar
300 ml/1¹/₄ cups brandy
125 g/¹/₂ cup gluten-free suet/shortening
100 g/1 cup unsalted pistachios, chopped
1 teaspoon ground cinnamon
1 teaspoon ground mixed spice/apple pie spice

For the pastry

50 g/3 tablespoons butter
190 g/1¹/₂ cups gluten-free plain/all-purpose flour, plus extra for dusting
60 g/¹/₄ cup plus 1 tablespoon caster/superfine sugar, plus extra for sprinkling
1 egg yolk
50 g/¹/₄ cup cream cheese
1 teaspoon ground cinnamon

To assemble

3 tablespoons cream cheese
grated zest of 1 orange
milk, for glazing
icing/confectioners' sugar, for dusting

3 sterilized glass jars with lids

8-cm/3-in round cookie cutter

12-hole muffin tin/pan, greased

Makes 12

mince pies with pistachio mincemeat

Although mincemeat is readily available in the supermarkets it can often contain wheat, so if you have time before Christmas, why not make your own gluten–free version? Check the packets of dried mixed fruit and suet carefully, to ensure they are gluten–free.

First make the mincemeat. Place all the ingredients in a large bowl and stir well with a spoon to make sure everything is mixed. Cover the bowl with a kitchen towel, then leave to stand for 1 hour to allow the flavours to develop. Transfer the mincemeat to a saucepan, and warm over low heat, until the suet/shortening has melted and the apple is cooked. Decant into sterilized jars, and seal with airtight lids. The mincemeat will keep for up to 1 year. You will need 1 jar for this recipe.

Preheat the oven to 180°C (350°F) Gas 4.

To make the pastry, cut the butter into small cubes, and rub it into the flour with your fingertips, until the mixture resembles fine breadcrumbs. Add the sugar, egg yolk, cream cheese and cinnamon, and mix together to a soft dough, adding a little cold water if the mixture is too dry.

On a flour-dusted surface, roll out the pastry to a 3 mm/¹/₁₆ inch thickness. Stamp out 24 pastry rounds using the cookie cutter, and press half of the rounds into the holes of the muffin tin/pan. Do not worry if the pastry cracks; simply patch with pastry trimmings. If you like, press the remaining rounds on to a star-shaped mould, to create a decorative imprint. These will be the tops. Fill each pastry case with a spoonful of mincemeat, top with a teaspoon of cream cheese and a little orange zest, then add the tops, pressing the pastry down gently. Using a pastry brush, brush the top of each pie with milk, and sprinkle with a little caster/superfne sugar.

Bake for 10–15 minutes in the preheated oven, until the pastry is golden brown. Remove the pies from the tin/pan while still warm. It is easiest to do this by pushing a teaspoon down the side of each pie. Transfer the pies to a wire rack to cool. Dust with icing/confectioners' sugar to serve. These pies will keep for up to 3 days in an airtight container.

For the cookie shell
300 g/10 oz. gluten-free
  gingernuts/gingersnaps
100 g/6 1/2 tablespoons butter,
  melted

For the pumpkin Chantilly
250 g/1 cup pumpkin purée
3 egg yolks and 4 egg whites
110 g/generous 1/2 cup
  caster/superfine sugar
250 ml/1 cup milk
1/2 teaspoon salt
1 teaspoon vanilla bean paste
1 teaspoon ground ginger
a pinch of grated nutmeg
1 teaspoon ground cinnamon
2 tablespoons melted butter
10 g/1 1/2 tablespoons
  powdered gelatine
60 ml/1/4 cup warm water

For the topping
80 g/1/3 cup caster/
  superfine sugar
50 g/1/3 cup shelled pecans
250 ml/1 cup double/heavy
  cream

blender or food processor

*23-cm/9-in round springform
cake tin/pan, greased and lined
with baking parchment*

*silicon mat or baking sheet,
greased*

Serves 10

pumpkin and pecan chiffon pie

My friend Marie Globus makes the best chiffon pumpkin pie.
Unlike traditional pumpkin pie, which can be quite heavy, this
spectacular festive dessert is light and airy.

For the cookie shell, blitz the gingernuts/gingersnaps to fine crumbs in a blender or
food processor, and add the melted butter. Stir well so that all the crumbs are coated
in butter. Press the crumbs into the prepared cake tin/pan using the back of a spoon
so that they cover the entire base and come about 3 cm/1 1/4 inches up the sides of
the tin/pan in a thin layer.

For the pumpkin Chantilly, place the pumpkin purée in a heatproof bowl over a
saucepan of simmering water, and heat for 10 minutes, stirring occasionally, to evaporate
some of the moisture. Add the 3 egg yolks, 50 g/1/4 cup of the caster/superfine sugar,
milk, salt, vanilla bean paste, ginger, nutmeg, cinnamon and melted butter to the bowl,
and whisk together. Cook for a further 10 minutes over the saucepan, then remove
from the heat.

Dissolve the powdered gelatine in the warm water, whisking well. Whisk the dissolved
gelatine into the pumpkin mixture, then leave to cool. Whisk the 4 egg whites to stiff
peaks and then fold in the remaining 60 g/generous 1/4 cup of caster/superfine sugar
a little at a time. Gently fold the egg white mixture into the pumpkin mixture, until
fully incorporated. Pour into the cookie shell. Allow to set in the refrigerator overnight.

For the topping, heat the sugar in a pan over low heat, until it melts and starts to
turn golden. Do not stir the sugar, but swirl the saucepan over the heat from time
to time to ensure even cooking. Watch carefully as when the sugar melts it can easily
burn. Spread the pecans out on the silicon mat or a greased baking sheet and swirl
over the melted sugar in pretty patterns, coating the pecans. Leave to set. These are
best made shortly before serving as they become sticky when exposed to the air.

To serve, carefully slide a knife around the edge of the tin/pan to release the cake.
Whip the cream to stiff peaks, and arrange it over the top of the pumpkin Chantilly,
forming soft peaks. Top with the caramelized pecans, and serve immediately.

spiced stollen

Stollen is a rich fruit bread, originating from 14th-century Germany. My version is bursting with cherries, chocolate and marzipan, with an amaretto and lemon dough.

250 g/2 cups gluten-free self-raising/self-rising flour, sifted (see Note, page 24)

1 tablespoon gluten-free baking powder

1 teaspoon xanthan gum

3 eggs, beaten

75 g/5 tablespoons butter, melted and cooled

300 ml/1¼ cups sour/soured cream

100 g/½ cup caster/superfine sugar

grated zest of 1 lemon

2 tablespoons amaretto or other almond liqueur

a pinch of vanilla salt (or 1 teaspoon pure vanilla extract and a pinch of salt)

200 g/1⅓ cups dried morello/tart cherries

100 g/⅔ cup unsalted pistachios, chopped

100 g/3½ oz. dark/bittersweet chocolate (70% cocoa solids), chopped

250 g/8 oz. golden marzipan

icing/confectioners' sugar, for dusting

38 x 13-cm/15 x 5-in stollen pan, very well greased

large baking sheet, greased and lined with baking parchment

Makes 1 large loaf

Preheat the oven to 180°C (350°F) Gas 4.

Sift the flour, baking powder and xanthan gum into a bowl. Add the eggs with 50 g/3 tablespoons of the melted butter, sour/soured cream and caster/superfine sugar. Stir in the lemon zest, amaretto, salt, cherries, pistachios and chopped chocolate. Spoon half of the mixture into the prepared stollen pan.

On a clean surface, use your hands to roll the marzipan out into a sausage shape the length of your stollen pan and place in the centre of the dough in the tin. Spoon the remaining dough mixture over the top of the marzipan, then invert on to the prepared baking sheet, keeping the stollen pan over the dough. (If you do not have a stollen pan, dust your hands with flour, and shape the dough into a long oval loaf, approximately 35 x 20 cm/14 x 8 inches, and insert the marzipan in the centre of the dough before shaping.

Bake for 40–50 minutes in the preheated oven, until the top is golden brown, gently lifting away the stollen pan to see if it is cooked. Remove the stollen from the oven and remove the pan.

Brush the top of the warm loaf with the remaining melted butter, and dust with icing/confectioners' sugar. The sugar will be absorbed by the butter, giving the loaf a sweet coating. This stollen is lovely eaten warm, spread with butter, if you wish, but will store well for up to 3 days in an airtight container. It can also be frozen in slices.

brandy snap baskets with spiced syllabub

Brandy snaps always remind me of childhood Christmases. Here the snaps are shaped into baskets (a true 1970s throwback for which I make no apologies), filled with a festive syllabub, scented with cinnamon, lemon and ginger, and topped with shimmering gold leaf.

For the brandy snap baskets
60 g/5 tablespoons butter
60 g/5 tablespoons caster/
superfine sugar
60 g/¼ cup golden/
light corn syrup
60 g/½ cup gluten-free plain/
all-purpose flour, sifted

For the syllabub
120 ml/½ cup green
ginger wine
grated zest and freshly
squeezed juice of 1 lemon
80 g/⅓ cup caster/
superfine sugar
1 teaspoon ground cinnamon
300 ml/1¼ cups double/
heavy cream
1 egg white

To serve
unsalted pistachios,
finely chopped
edible gold leaf

*large baking sheet, lined
with a silicon mat*

palette knife

*4 glass tumblers, greased
with butter*

Serves 8

Preheat the oven to 180°C (350°F) Gas 4.

For the brandy snap baskets, heat the butter, sugar and syrup in a saucepan over a gentle heat, until the butter has melted and the sugar has dissolved. Remove the saucepan from the heat, and stir in the flour. Place four large spoonfuls of the mixture on the prepared baking sheet, placing them a large distance apart as they will spread during cooking.

Bake for 10–12 minutes in the preheated oven, until the cookies turn a golden orange colour. Remove from the oven and allow to set for a few minutes on the baking sheet. They should be firm enough to move without stretching, but still flexible enough to shape. If they set too hard, simply return to the oven for a minute to soften.

Using a palette knife, lift each cookie over the base of a prepared glass tumbler, and press down so that the cookie takes the shape of the glass and makes a basket. Leave on the glass until cool. Repeat the above steps with the remaining batter to make a further 4 baskets. The baskets will store in an airtight container for up to 5 days.

For the syllabub, place the wine, lemon zest and juice, sugar and cinnamon in a bowl, and leave to soak for 1 hour, until the sugar dissolves, stirring occasionally. Place the sugar syrup in a mixing bowl with the double/heavy cream, and whip to stiff peaks.

Place the egg white in a separate clean bowl, and whisk to stiff peaks. Gently fold the egg white into the cream mixture. Divide the syllabub between the brandy snap baskets, sprinkle with pistachios and top with a little gold leaf. Serve immediately.

great grandma's christmas pudding

Making Christmas puddings is one of my family traditions. We make the Christmas puddings in my Great Grandma's crock pot, and this is my gluten-free version of our recipe.

250 g/1 cup gluten-free
   suet/shortening
350 g/2^1/$_2$ cups (dark) raisins
225 g/1^1/$_2$ cups sultanas/
   golden raisins
225 g/1^1/$_2$ cups currants
225 g/1 cup caster/
   superfine sugar
85 g/^{3}/$_4$ cup ground almonds
140 g/1 cup gluten-free
   self-raising/self-rising flour,
   sifted (see Note, page 24)
1 large apple, peeled,
   cored and grated
1 large carrot, peeled
   and grated
3 large/US extra large eggs
grated zest and freshly
   squeezed juice of
   1 lemon and 1 orange
^{1}/$_4$ teaspoon grated nutmeg
1 teaspoon ground mixed
   spice/apple pie spice
a pinch of salt
200 ml/^{3}/$_4$ cup apple cider
2 tablespoons brandy, plus
   extra for flambéing

2 pudding basins/deep
heat-proof bowls, greased

baking parchment, foil and
kitchen twine

large steamer pan

Makes 2 puddings

Place all the ingredients in a large mixing bowl and stir well. Make sure that everyone in your house stirs the mixture 3 times and makes a wish! Cover with a kitchen towel, and leave in a cool place for 24 hours to allow the flavours to develop.

Divide the mixture between 2 prepared pudding basins, leaving a gap of a centimetre or so between the mixture and the top of each basin. Cover the tops of the basins with a double layer of baking parchment, with a pleat folded in to allow for expansion as the pudding cooks, and secure the paper in place with kitchen twine. Cover the paper with a layer of foil, and fold the edges of the foil tightly under the rim of the basin in a pleating motion. Tie string round the top rim of the basin, and over the top to make a handle, so that the pudding can be lifted out of the steamer pan easily.

The puddings need to be steamed for at least 7 hours each, but this can be done in stages, whenever you have time. Keep the puddings in the fridge in between cooking sessions. I find that the longer they are cooked, the better flavour they have. To steam the pudding, place the pudding in a steamer pan or in a steamer basket above a pan of simmering water and cover with a lid. Check the water regularly, refilling as necessary. The pudding should be a dark brown colour. Once cooked, the puddings will keep in the refrigerator for up to 1 year.

When you are ready to eat the pudding, steam it in the pudding basin for a further hour, to ensure that it is warmed all the way through. To serve, remove the baking parchment and foil, and slide a knife carefully around the edge of the basin. Place a plate on top of the basin and invert, holding both the plate and the basin tightly.

To flambé, heat 1 tablespoon of brandy in a large spoon over a flame. It will ignite as it heats, so be ready to quickly tip it over the pudding when it does, and serve immediately with brandy butter and brandy sauce.

For the trifle sponge

5 eggs

140 g/^{2}/3 cup caster/superfine sugar, plus extra for sprinkling

a pinch of vanilla salt (or 1 teaspoon pure vanilla extract and a pinch of salt)

100 g/^{2}/3 cup gluten-free self-raising/self-rising flour (see Note, page 24)

1 teaspoon gluten-free baking powder

60 g/^{2}/3 cup ground almonds

4 tablespoons raspberry jam/jelly

For the fruit

350 g/2^1/2 cup blueberries

1 tablespoon caster/superfine sugar

300 g/2 cups raspberries

To assemble

125 ml/^{1}/2 cup brandy

125 ml/^{1}/2 cup sherry

500 ml/2 cups custard

400 ml/1^2/3 cups double/heavy cream, whipped to soft peaks

pomegranate seeds

Swiss roll tin/jelly roll pan

baking parchment

large glass dish

Serves 10

proper sherry trifle

Christmas wouldn't be Christmas without a beautiful centrepiece trifle. The base of this trifle is made with a gluten-free Swiss roll/jelly roll, swirled with raspberry jam, which looks very pretty.

Preheat the oven to 180°C (350°F) Gas 4.

For the sponge, whisk together the eggs, caster/superfine sugar and vanilla salt in a large mixing bowl for 3–5 minutes, using an electric mixer, until thick, creamy and pale. Sift together the flour and baking powder in a separate bowl, add the ground almonds, and fold into the egg mixture using a spatula. Fold very gently, otherwise you will lose all the air whipped into the eggs, which gives the roll its light texture.

Spoon the mixture into the Swiss roll tin/jelly roll pan and bake for 5 minutes in the preheated oven, then turn the tin around and cook for a further 3–5 minutes, until the sponge is golden brown and feels just firm to your touch. Sprinkle a generous amount of caster/superfine sugar on to a sheet of baking parchment. Turn the sponge out on to the sugar-dusted sheet, and cover with a clean damp kitchen towel. Leave for 5 minutes.

Remove the kitchen towel. Mix the jam with a spoon, so that it is easily spreadable, then spread it over the sponge. Roll up the sponge from one of the long ends (as you want to make small swirls of sponge), using the sugar-dusted parchment to guide the sponge. Leave the Swiss roll/jelly roll wrapped in the parchment, until cool.

Simmer half of the blueberries in a saucepan with 60 ml/^{1}/4 cup water and the caster/superfine sugar for 5 minutes, until the fruit is soft and the liquid is syrupy. Allow to cool.

To assemble your trifle, cut the roll into slices and press into the base and sides of your dish. Drizzle over the brandy and sherry – adding more if you like. Spoon the blueberry compote on to the base of the trifle, then sprinkle over the remaining blueberries and raspberries. Spoon over the custard, then top with a layer of whipped cream. Sprinkle with the pomegranate seeds. Chill for at least 3 hours before serving. The trifle will keep for 3 days, covered in the refrigerator.

For the cake

400 g/14 oz. dried mixed fruit
100 g/²/₃ cup glacé/candied
    cherries, halved
200 ml/³/₄ cup ginger wine
1 tablespoon brandy, plus
    extra for feeding (optional)
225 g/2 sticks butter, softened
225 g/1 generous cup soft
    dark brown sugar
4 eggs, beaten
140 g/1 generous cup
    gluten-free self-raising/
    self-rising flour, sifted
    (see Note, page 24)
2 teaspoons baking powder
115 g/1 heaped cup ground
    almonds
1 teaspoon ground cinnamon
1 teaspoon ground mixed
    spice/apple pie spice
1 teaspoon pure vanilla
    extract

To decorate

250 g/8 oz. golden marzipan
3 tablespoons smooth
    apricot jam/jelly
300 g/10 oz. ready-to-roll
    icing/fondant
icing/confectioners' sugar,
    for dusting
red gluten-free sugar candies

*23-cm/9-in round loose-bottomed
springform cake tin/pan, greased
and lined with baking parchment*

holly cutter

ribbon

Serves 8–12

last-minute christmas fruit cake

This is a great cake to make if you discover at the last minute that you have someone with a wheat allergy visiting for Christmas. As the fruit is soaked in wine and brandy until plump there is no need to 'feed' the cake with alcohol, unless you wish to.

Put the mixed fruit, cherries, ginger wine and brandy in a bowl, cover and soak overnight.

Preheat the oven to 160°C (325°F) Gas 3. Whisk together the butter and sugar, until light and creamy. Whisk in the eggs. Add the flour, baking powder, almonds, cinnamon, mixed spice and vanilla, as well as the fruit and soaking liquid. Mix until incorporated.

Spoon the mixture into the prepared cake tin/pan and bake for about 1¹/₂ hours, until the cake springs back to your touch and a skewer comes out clean when inserted into the middle of the cake. Leave the cake to cool in the tin for a few minutes, then turn out and place on a wire rack to cool completely. If you want to 'feed' your cake, pierce small holes in the top and spoon over a few tablespoons of brandy.

When you are ready to serve, dust a surface with icing/confectioners' sugar, and roll out the marzipan to a 5 mm/¹/₄ inch thickness. Using the washed and dried base of the cake tin as a template, cut out a 23-cm/9-inch circle of marzipan. Gently heat the apricot jam in a saucepan, and brush over the top of the cake using a pastry brush. Using a rolling pin, lift the marzipan circle on to the cake and press down.

Roll out 250 g/8 oz. of the ready-to-roll icing/fondant and cut out a 23-cm/9-inch circle, using the same method as above. Brush the top of the marzipan with more apricot jam, and place the icing circle on top. Crimp the edges of the ready-to-roll icing and marzipan into pretty patterns. Roll out the remaining icing, and cut out holly leaves. Fix the holly leaves to the top of the cake using a little of the apricot jam and tie a ribbon around the edge of the cake. Add red candy 'berries'.

The cake will keep for up to 5 days in an airtight container. Alternatively, wrap the un-iced cake in baking parchment and clingfilm/plastic wrap and store in an airtight container. Unwrap the cake and 'feed' it with several spoonfuls of brandy each week.

tunis cake

This cake is often served at Christmas in place of a traditional iced fruit cake. It is a light, lemon Madeira sponge and is perfect for those who find fruit cake a little heavy. Decorated with marzipan fruits, this cake makes a perfect centrepiece for a Christmas buffet table.

For the cake
225 g/1 cup caster/
    superfine sugar
225 g/2 sticks butter,
    softened
4 eggs
grated zest of 2 lemons
140 g/1 generous cup
    gluten-free self-raising/
    self-rising flour, sifted
2 teaspoons gluten-free
    baking powder
115 g/1 generous cup
    ground almonds
2 tablespoons milk

**For the chocolate
    ganache**
200 g/7 oz. plain/
    semisweet chocolate,
    broken into pieces
2 tablespoons glucose or
    golden/light corn syrup
120 ml/¹/₂ cup double/
    heavy cream
2 tablespoons butter

To decorate
gluten-free marzipan fruits

*23-cm/9-in round springform
cake tin/pan, greased and lined
with baking parchment*

Serves 10

Preheat the oven to 180°C (350°F) Gas 4.

For the cake, whisk together the sugar and butter in a mixing bowl, until light and creamy. Beat the eggs into the mixture, one by one, and then gently fold in the lemon zest, flour, baking powder, ground almonds and milk.

Spoon the mixture into the prepared cake tin/pan, and bake in the preheated oven for 40–50 minutes, until the cake is golden brown and springs back to your touch, and a knife inserted into the centre of the cake comes out clean. If the cake starts to brown too much before it is completely cooked, cover it with a layer of foil. Turn the cake out on to a wire rack to cool completely.

For the ganache, place the chocolate, glucose or syrup, cream and butter in a heatproof bowl placed over a pan of simmering water, and heat until the chocolate and butter have melted. It is important that the bottom of the bowl does not touch the water. Stir well, until you have a thick glossy chocolate sauce.

Spoon the chocolate ganache over the top of the cake, and decorate with the marzipan fruits. This cake will keep for up to 2 days if stored in an airtight container.

sauces & stuffings

tarator walnut sauce

This is one of my favourite sauces to serve with fish or roasted chicken, great for festive buffets. Its origins are Mediterranean and the delicious flavours work very well with Christmas turkey.

200 g/1 1/3 cups walnuts
3–4 slices of gluten-free bread
1–2 garlic cloves, peeled and finely chopped
juice of 1–2 lemons
100 ml/6 tablespoons olive oil, plus extra to serve
100 ml/6 tablespoons natural set yogurt
salt and freshly ground black pepper, to season

baking sheet

food processor

Serves 6–8

Preheat the oven to 180°C (350°F) Gas 4.

Place the walnuts on the baking sheet and bake in the preheated oven for about 3–5 minutes, until the nuts just start to colour and their oils are released. Watch carefully during cooking so that the nuts do not burn. Shake the sheet occasionally to ensure even cooking. Remove the nuts from the oven and leave to cool.

Soak the bread in a little water until it is soft. Place the roasted nuts, soaked bread, garlic and the juice of 1 of the lemons in a food processor, and blitz to a smooth paste. Add the oil and yogurt, and blitz again. Season with salt and pepper, and add a little more lemon juice, to taste. Drizzle with a little extra olive oil to serve. This sauce will keep for up to 2 days in the refrigerator, but is best served on the day it is made.

cranberry sauce

This sauce is perfect with turkey. It has a tangy taste with a peppery kick of ginger from the ginger wine. It can be served warm or cold, whichever you prefer, and keeps well in sterilized jars in the refrigerator.

600 g/6 cups cranberries
125 ml/1/2 cup green ginger wine
1 cinnamon stick
250 ml/1 cup water
100 g/1/2 cup white/granulated sugar
salt and freshly ground black pepper
grated zest and freshly squeezed juice of large orange

Makes 2 jars

Place all the ingredients in a saucepan and simmer over a gentle heat for about 20–30 minutes, until the sauce is thick and the cranberries have burst. Remove the cinnamon stick before serving.

If you wish to store the cranberry sauce, spoon it into sterilized jars and keep in the refrigerator for up to 3 months. Alternatively, you can freeze the sauce and defrost before using.

bread sauce

For me, turkey just can't be eaten without bread sauce. With the main component being bread, it is often off the menu for those allergic to gluten. This is my gluten-free version, and it is just as tasty as the original.

20 whole cloves
1 large shallot
500 ml/2 cups milk
300 ml/1 1/4 cups double/
    heavy cream
2 bay leaves
a pinch of grated nutmeg

6–8 slices of gluten-free
    bread, cut into pieces
2 tablespoons butter
salt and freshly ground
    black pepper

Serves 6–8

Carefully press the whole cloves into the shallot. Place the clove-studded shallot in a saucepan with the milk, cream and bay leaves, and season with salt, pepper and a little nutmeg. Heat the milk mixture over medium-high heat and bring to the boil. As soon as it boils, remove it from the heat and set aside for 30 minutes, so that the flavours of the shallot and spices can infuse into the milk.

Strain the milk over a large bowl, and discard the shallot and bay leaves. Return the milk to the pan. Add the bread pieces to the pan and simmer over low heat until the sauce becomes thick and the bread absorbs the milk mixture. Add more bread, if needed, until the sauce is thick. Add the butter to the pan and stir until it has melted. Taste for seasoning, and serve warm.

festive gravy

Christmas is one of those occasions when it is definitely worth taking the time to make proper gravy. It freezes well so you can prepare it ahead of time, if you wish. This is a rich gravy, and is perfect with turkey!

1 large onion, peeled and
    finely chopped
1 tablespoon olive oil
2 tablespoons butter
300 ml/1 1/4 cups Madeira
    or sweet sherry
100 ml/6 tablespoons
    brandy
800 ml/3 1/3 cups chicken
    or turkey stock

2 tablespoons cornflour/
    cornstarch
salt and freshly ground
    black pepper
200 ml/3/4 cups
    double/heavy cream
    (optional)

Serves 6–8

Place the finely chopped onion in a saucepan with the olive oil and 1 tablespoon of the butter. Season with salt and pepper, and simmer over a gentle heat until the onions are soft and translucent, and are just starting to caramelize. Add the Madeira and brandy, and simmer for 15–20 minutes, until the liquid has reduced by about half.

When the liquid is thick and syrupy, add the stock to the pan and continue to simmer until the liquid has reduced by one-third. In a small bowl rub the remaining butter into the cornflour/cornstarch with your fingertips. Add to the saucepan, a little at a time, whisking constantly until the sauce thickens. Alternatively, for a thinner, richer gravy, add 200 ml/3/4 cups of double/heavy cream instead of the butter and cornflour/cornstarch. Season well, and serve hot.

chestnut forcemeat stuffing balls

For me, Christmas lunch wouldn't be complete without generous helpings of sausage meat stuffing. It is important that you use gluten-free sausage meat in the recipe – I find it best to use gluten-free sausages and simply remove the skins.

400 g/14 oz. gluten-free pork
    sausages, skins removed
1 small/US medium
    egg, beaten
200 g/6–8 oz. chestnuts,
    peeled
90 g/3 oz. sliced gluten-free
    bread
1 tablespoon fresh
    flat-leaf parsley
salt and freshly ground
    black pepper
olive oil, for drizzling

blender or food processor

roasting pan

Makes 15 balls

Preheat the oven to 200°C (400°F) Gas 6.

Place the sausage meat from the sausages in a mixing bowl, and stir in the beaten egg. Place the chestnuts, bread and parsley in a blender or food processor, and blitz to fine crumbs. Season with salt and pepper.

Mix the chestnut, bread and parsley crumbs into the sausage mixture. This is best done with clean hands to ensure that everything is mixed in, squashing the mixture together with your fingers.

Divide the sausage mixture into 15 even pieces, and roll them into small balls between your hands. Place them in the roasting pan, drizzle with a little olive oil, and bake in the preheated oven for 25–30 minutes, until the balls are golden brown on the outside and cooked through. To check if they are cooked, cut one ball in half and check that the sausage meat is no longer pink on the inside. Serve immediately.